CH00762323

Get Right with TAO

A CONTEMPORARY SPIN
ON THE TAO TE CHING

RON HOGAN

Channel V Books
New York

Channel V Books
New York

Interior and cover design: Susan Lindberg

Published in the United States by Channel V Books,
a division of Channel V Media, New York, NY.
www.ChannelVBooks.com

Channel V Books and its logo are trademarks of Channel V Media.
ISBN 978-0-9824739-8-6
Library of Congress Control Number: 2010921122

Library of Congress subject headings:
Laozi. – Dao de jing. – English.

PRINTED IN THE UNITED STATES OF AMERICA
10 9 8 7 6 5 4 3 2 1

First Edition

For Laura

●

C O N T E N T S

INTRODUCTION

BEFORE WE GO ANY FURTHER, let's make one thing clear:
This is not the Tao Te Ching.

Though frequently characterized as a religious text due to its central
role in Taoist philosophy, Tao Te Ching is, perhaps, the world's first
great self-help book. (One very rough translation of the title might
be "The Great Book of the Way of Integrity.") We don't know much
about its origins, other than that it predates the birth of Christianity
by several centuries. The text is attributed to Lao Tzu—as legend has
it, he was a bureaucrat in the royal court who became disgusted by
public and private corruption and decided to leave, but was stopped
at the border by a guard who begged him to write down some of
his teachings for posterity. Some scholars, though, will tell you that
he isn't even a real person; others will tell you he's real but not
everything people say about him is.

In any event: The Tao Te Ching (let's abbreviate it to TTC from here)
is a product of ancient Chinese culture, written in a style that would
have been perfectly transparent to someone from that period, relying
on imagery and metaphors they would have instantly recognized.
For a modern reader, though, some of those references may not be as
straightforward. When I first read the TTC in my mid-twenties, in
the translation by Stephen Mitchell, it was a little too refined for my
tastes, too much "wisdom of the ancients." (That said, it's still a highly
accessible translation, and worth reading!)

I was (and am) a huge David Mamet fan, so I imagined a TTC that was as plain and as intense as his dialogue. I started looking at other translations to see how they expressed Lao Tzu's philosophy, and while I didn't find anybody who was putting it into the language I wanted to read, I discovered that translators were giving themselves a lot of poetic license. If you don't actually know Chinese, you're pretty much at the mercy of somebody else's idea of what Lao Tzu was saying—and some of those "translators" are upfront about not knowing the language very well themselves.

I know absolutely no Chinese.

As I said, this isn't the Tao Te Ching. Instead of translating from the Chinese, I took a lot of different English-language versions, somewhere between 12 and 20, and sorted out what underlying ideas each version had in common, then rewrote those ideas in my own voice, a voice that might be more easily recognizable to contemporary Americans than Lao Tzu's.

As I see it, the true power of the TTC isn't the poetic language, but the practical wisdom—Lao Tzu's guidelines for how to live an authentic life, one day at a time. So that's what I aimed for.

There's a long story behind how it took me nearly a decade, off and on, to finish that project, and I've told that story as part of the introduction to an earlier version which I published online and let people download for free—over the years, more than 100,000 people took me up on that offer. Recently, though, I started thinking about how cool it would be to have a version in print, and that tied in neatly with another idea I had about a new project that would continue my interest in personal development and take it to a new level. (You'll find out more about it at the end of the book.)

I used this opportunity to take another pass at the text, to see if I've gotten any better at expressing myself in the half-decade since I last played with Lao Tzu's idea. If you're familiar with the online version, you won't find any real surprises here, but there are enough little tweaks that I felt it was time for a new title, and I turned to a phrase that I used frequently: *Getting Right with Tao.* It gets at the heart of what I think the Tao Te Ching is about: Lao Tzu was inviting readers to initiate a process, revealing how life is an ongoing series of opportunities to do the right thing. It's not an easy process, but it can make our lives so much easier if we follow through on it. And if we make mistakes, we can always start again.

Just remember: That's *my* idea of what Lao Tzu was saying, and I've made some major changes along the way. For example, Lao Tzu never said, "Don't spend too much time thinking about stupid shit." I've included some information in the back of the book about other translations that stick closer to the original message. Overall, though, I've tried to stay true to the core of Lao Tzu's advice, which has been very helpful to me over the last fifteen years when I've been clearheaded enough to remember it, and I hope it will be helpful to you, too.

—Ron Hogan
New York, February 2010

PART ONE

TAO
(the way)

●

1

If you can talk about it,
it ain't Tao.
If it has a name, it's just another thing.

Tao doesn't have a name.
Names are for ordinary things.

Stop wanting stuff; it keeps you from seeing what's real.
When you want stuff, all you see are things.

Those two sentences mean the same thing.
Figure them out, and you've got it made.

●

2

If something looks beautiful to you, something else must be ugly.
If something seems right, you're calling something else wrong.

You can't have something without nothing.
If no job is difficult,
then no job is easy.
Some things are up high
because other things are down low.
You know you're listening to music
because it doesn't sound like noise.
All that came first, so this must be next.

The Masters get the job done
without moving a muscle
and get their point across
without saying a word.

When things around them fall apart, they stay cool.
They don't own much, but they use whatever's at hand.
They do the work without expecting any favors.
When they're done, they move on to the next job.
That's why their work is so damn good.

●

3

If you toss compliments around freely,
people will waste your time trying to impress you.
If you give things too much value, you're going to get ripped off.
If you try to please people, you'll wind up pissing them off.

The Master leads by clearing the crap
out of people's heads and opening their hearts.
He lowers their aspirations and makes them suck in their guts.

He shows you how to forget what you know and what you want,
so nobody can push you around.
If you think you've got the answers, he'll mess with your head.

Stop doing stuff all the time,
and watch what happens.

●

4

How much Tao is there?
More than you'll ever need.
Use all you want,
there's plenty more where that came from.

You can't see Tao, but it's there.
Damned if I know where it came from.
It's just always been around.

●

5

Tao's neutral: It doesn't worry about good or evil.
The Masters are neutral: They treat everyone the same.

Lao Tzu said Tao is like a bellows:
It's empty, but it could help set the world on fire.
If you keep using Tao, it works better.
If you keep talking about it, it won't make any sense.

Be cool.

●

6

Tao is an eternal mystery,
and everything starts with Tao.

Everybody has Tao in them.
They just have to use it.

●

7

Tao never stops. Why?
Because it isn't trying to accomplish anything.

The Masters hang back.
That's why they're ahead of the game.

They don't hang on to things.
That's how they manage to keep them.

They don't worry about what they can't control.
That's why they're always satisfied.

●

8

"Doing the right thing" is like water.
It's good for all living things,
and flows without thinking about where it's going

...just like Tao.

Keep your feet on the ground.
Remember what's important.
Be there when people need you.
Say what you mean.
Be prepared for anything.
Do what you can, when it needs doing.

If you don't compare yourself to others,
nobody can compare to you.

●

9

If you drink too much, you get drunk.
The engine won't start if you're always tinkering with it.

If you hoard wealth, you fall into its clutches.
If you crave success, you succumb to failure.

Do what you have to do, then walk away.
Anything else will drive you nuts.

●

1 0

Can you hold on to your ego
and still stay focused on Tao?

Can you relax your mind and body,
and brace yourself for a new life?

Can you check yourself and see past what's in front of your eyes?

Can you be a leader and not try to prove you're in charge?

Can you deal with what's happening and let it happen?

Can you forget what you know and understand what's real?

Start a job and see it through.
Have things without holding on to them.
Do the job without expectation of reward.
Lead people without giving orders.
That's the way you do it.

●

1 1

A wheel has spokes,
but it rotates around a hollow center.

A pot is made of clay or glass,
but you keep things in the space inside.

A house is made of wood or brick,
but you live between the walls.

We work with something, but we use nothing.

●

12

Sight obscures.
Noise deafens.

Desire messes with your heart.
The world messes with your mind.

A Master watches the world,
but keeps focused on what's real.

●

13

Winning can be just as bad as losing.
Confidence can mess you up just as much as fear.

What does "winning can be just as bad as losing" mean?

If you're down, you might be able to get up.
But if you're up, you can get knocked down really fast.
Don't worry about the score.
Just do what you have to do.

What does "confidence can mess you up just as much as fear" mean?

Fear can keep you from getting the job done,
but confidence can get you in over your head.
Walk tall, but don't get cocky.

Know your limits, and nothing can ever hold you back.
Deal with what you can.
The rest will follow.

●

1 4

You can't see Tao,
no matter how hard you look.
You can't hear Tao,
no matter how hard you listen.
You can't hold on to Tao,
no matter how hard you grab.

But it's there.

It's in you, and it's all around you.

Remember that.

●

1 5

The ancient Masters were damn impressive.
They were deep. Really deep.
Words can't even begin to describe how deep they were.
You can only talk about how they acted.

They were careful, like a man walking on thin ice.
They were cautious, like a soldier behind enemy lines.
They were polite, like a guest at a party.
They moved quickly, like melting ice.
They were as plain as a block of wood.
Their minds were as wide as a valley,
and their hearts as clear as spring water.

Can you wait for that kind of openness and clarity
before you try to understand the world?

Can you hold still until events have unfolded
before you do the right thing?

When you act without expectations,
you can accomplish great things.

16

Keep your head clear.
Stay calm.
Watch as everything happens around you.

Everything reverts to its original state,
which was nothing.
And when something becomes nothing,
it gets right with Tao.

If you don't understand that,
you're going to screw up somewhere down the line.
If you figure it out, you'll always know what to do.

If you get right with Tao,
you won't be afraid to die,
because you know you will.

●

17

When a Master takes charge, hardly anybody notices.
The next best leader is obeyed out of love.
After that, there's the leader obeyed out of fear.
The worst leader is one who is hated.

Trust and respect people.
That's how you earn their trust and respect.

The Masters don't give orders; they work with everybody else.
When the job's done, people are amazed
at what they accomplished.

●

18

When people lose touch with Tao,
they start talking about "righteousness" and "sanctity."

When people forget what's true,
they start talking about "self-evident truths."

When people have no respect for one another,
they start talking about "political correctness" and "family values."

When the nation is unstable,
people start talking about "patriotism."

●

19

Get rid of sanctity.
People will understand the truth and be happier.

Get rid of morality.
People will respect each other and do what's right.

Get rid of value and profit.
People will not steal if they do not desire.

If that's not possible, go to Plan B:
Be simple. Be real.
Do your work as best you can.
Don't think about what you get for it.
Stay focused. Get rid of all your crap.

●

2 0

Don't spend too much time thinking about stupid shit.
Why should you care if people agree or disagree with you?
Why should you care if others find you attractive or not?
Why should you care about things that worry others?
Call bullshit on all that.

Let other people get worked up and try to enjoy themselves.
I'm not going to give myself away.
A baby doesn't know how to smile, but it's still happy.

Let other people get excited about stuff.
I'm not going to hang on to anything.
I'm not going to fill my mind with ideas.
I'm not going to get stuck in a rut, tied down to any one place.

Other people are clever;
I guess I must be stupid.
Other people have goals;
I guess I must be aimless.
Like the wind. Or the waves.

I'm not like other people.
I'm getting right with Tao.

●

21

A Master stays focused on Tao.
Nothing else, just Tao.

But you can't pin Tao down — you can't even see it!
How are you supposed to focus on something like that?

Just remember what Lao Tzu said:
The universe began as a void.
The void fills with images.
Images lead to the creation of objects.
And every object has Tao at its core.

That's the way it's been, since the world began.
How can I be so sure?
I just know.

●

2 2

Learn how to stand still if you want to go places.
Get on your knees if you want to stand tall.
If you want wisdom, empty your mind.
If you want the world, renounce your riches.
Push yourself until you're exhausted,
and then you'll find your strength.

You can go far if you don't have anything to carry.
The more you acquire, the less you can really appreciate.

A Master takes this to heart
and sets an example for everybody else.

She doesn't show off so people take notice.
She's not out to prove anything so people take her at her word.
She doesn't brag about herself but people know what she's done.
She hasn't got an agenda but people know what she can do.
She's not out to get anybody so nobody can get in her way.

"Learn how to stand still if you want to go places."
That's not as crazy as it sounds.
Get in touch with Tao, and you'll see what I mean.

●

23

When you have nothing to say,
you may as well keep your mouth shut.
The wind and the rain don't go on forever.
If nature knows enough to give it a rest sometimes,
so should you.

If you're ready for Tao, you can live with Tao.
If you're ready to succeed, you can live with success.
If you're ready to fail, you can live with failure.

Trust your instincts,
and others will trust you.

●

2 4

Keep your feet firmly planted unless you want to fall on your face.
Learn how to pace yourself if you want to get anywhere.
Don't call attention to yourself
if you want people to notice your work.

Nobody respects people who always have excuses.
Nobody gives credit to people who always take it.
People who hype themselves have nothing else to offer.

Think of being in touch with Tao like eating at a buffet:
Take only what you need.
Save some for everybody else.

●

25

There's something perfect that has existed forever,
even longer than the universe.
It's a vast, unchanging void.
There's nothing else like it.
It goes on forever and never stops, and everything else came from it.

I don't know what else to call it so I'll call it Tao.
What's it like?
I can tell you this much: It's great.

So great that it endures.
And something that endures goes a long way.
And something that goes a long way
always comes back to the beginning.

Tao's great.
Heaven's great.
Earth's great.
And someone in touch with Tao is great, too.
Those are the four greatest things in the universe.

Someone who's in touch with Tao is in touch with the earth.
The earth is in touch with heaven.
Heaven's in touch with Tao.
Tao's in touch with the way things are.

●

26

To be light on your feet, you need a steady mind.
If your body is active, your mind should be relaxed.

A Master can travel long distances and still see everything she owns.
She may be surrounded by beauty, but she isn't caught up in it.

Why run around thoughtlessly?
If you act lightly, you lose your bearings.
If you act recklessly, you lose your self-control.

●

2 7

With enough practice, you could come and go without a trace,
speak without stumbling over words,
and do complicated math problems in your head.

You could build a door with no lock that nobody could open.
You could tie something down with no knots, without even a rope,
and nobody could pry it loose.

Masters have time to help everybody, and ignore nobody.
They use their resources wisely, wasting nothing.
Some people call this "following the light."

Good people teach others because they have the potential to be good, too.
Brains count for nothing if you fail to respect your teachers
or to honor the potential in others.
That's one of the most important lessons of Tao.

28

If you are strong,
but remain sensitive,
power will flow through you.
With that power, you'll always be right with Tao:
It's like a whole new life.

If you are idealistic,
but stay rooted in reality,
you are an example to others.
Set that example, and you'll always be right with Tao:
There is no limit to what you can do.

If you are honorable,
but remain humble,
you will see things as they are.
If you see things as they are, you'll always be right with Tao:
Your life will become simple, yet full of potential.

Let Tao show you how to get right with Tao,
so your slightest gesture can change the world.

●

29

Want to take over the world? Think again.
The world's a holy place.
You can't just fuck around with it.
Those who try to change it destroy it.
Those who try to possess it lose it.

With Tao, you push forward, or maybe you stay behind.
Sometimes you push yourself, other times you rest.
Sometimes you're strong, sometimes you're weak.
Sometimes you're up, and sometimes you're down.

A Master lives simply, avoiding extravagance and excess.

●

3 0

Listen up: If you want to be a leader who's in touch with Tao, never use violence to achieve your goals.

Every act of violence backfires.
An army on the move leaves a trail of tears,
and a military victory always lies in ruins.

The Masters do what needs doing and that's all they do.
Do what you have to do without arrogance or pride.
Get the job done and don't brag about it afterwards.
Do what you have to do,
not for your own benefit,
but because it needs to be done.
And don't do it the way you think it should be done,
do it the way it needs to be done.

The mighty will always lose their power
and any connection they ever had to Tao.
They will not last long;
if you're not right with Tao, you might as well be dead.

●

3 1

Weapons are terrible things.
If you want to get right with Tao, reject weapons.

The Master, knowing all things came from Tao,
recognizes what he has in common with his enemies
and always tries to avoid conflict.

But when there is no other choice, he uses force reluctantly.
He does so with great restraint, and never celebrates a victory;
to do so would be to rejoice in killing.
A person who would rejoice in killing has completely lost touch with Tao.

When you win a war, you preside over a funeral.
Pay your respects to the dead.

●

3 2

Tao is an eternal mystery,
so small you can never take hold of it.

If a leader gets right with Tao, people will follow him on instinct.
All will be right with the world.
People will do the right thing without being told.

Everything that comes from Tao needs a name.
But once everything has its name,
you should make no other distinction between things.
That way, you won't be trapped by them.

Everything in the universe is full of Tao and leads to Tao,
just like the water in rivers that flows into oceans.

●

33

Knowing things makes you smart,
but knowing yourself makes you wise.
To rule others, you must be powerful,
but to rule yourself, you must be strong.

If you have only what you need, you have true wealth.
If you never give up, you will find a way.
If you stay true to yourself, you will never be lost.
If you stay alive your whole life, you've really lived.

●

34

Tao flows in all directions.
It's in everything, but nothing can contain it.
Everything needs Tao, so Tao provides,
and never expects anything in return.

Everything comes from Tao, but Tao doesn't call attention to itself.
It wants for nothing.
Think nothing of it.

Everything leads to Tao, but Tao doesn't call attention to itself.
Pretty impressive, huh?

It doesn't strive for success.
That's why it succeeds.

●

35

When you get right with Tao, everybody wants to be your friend.
When they're around you, they can relax and enjoy themselves.

People can be easily distracted by music or good food.
When we try to talk about Tao, it seems boring by comparison.

It doesn't look like much.
It doesn't sound like much.
But no matter how much you use, there's always plenty left.

36

To make something smaller, you need to appreciate its size.
To make something weaker, you must recognize its strength.
To get rid of something, you need to hold it tight.
To take something, you must give it up entirely.

To put it another way:
Sensitivity and weakness overcome unfeeling strength.

●

37

Tao never does anything but nothing is left undone.

If our leaders could get in touch with Tao,
the world would take care of itself.
Even if they wanted to impose their own ideas,
they'd be drawn back to Tao's nameless simplicity.

When our lives are that simple, we want for nothing.
We can relax, and the world becomes a better place.

PART TWO

TE
(integrity)

●

3 8

People with integrity don't even think about it.
That's how you can tell they have integrity.
Other people talk about how much integrity they have,
when they really don't have much. If any.

Truly powerful people don't do anything,
but they get the job done.
Other people are always busy doing something,
but nothing ever gets done.

When kind people act, they do so without thinking about it.
When the just act, they're always sure they're doing the right thing.
But when the righteous act, and nobody reacts,
they try to force everyone to do things their way.

If you're not in touch with Tao, at least you can still have integrity.
If you don't have integrity, there's always kindness.
If you don't have kindness, there's always justice.
If you don't have justice, all you have left is righteousness.

Righteousness is a pale imitation of true faith and loyalty,
and always leads to trouble.
If you've already made up your mind,
you don't know the first thing about Tao, and you never will.

The Masters pay attention to what's beneath the surface.
They'll look at a tree's leaves, but eat the fruit.
They turn all that down, so they can accept this.

●

39

Since time began, this is what it's meant
to be in touch with Tao:

Tao made the heavens clear.
Tao made the earth solid.
Tao made our spirits strong.
Tao made the valleys fertile.
Tao gave all living things life.
Tao gave rulers authority.

Without Tao, the heavens would collapse.
Without Tao, the earth would crumble.
Without Tao, our spirits would fade away.
Without Tao, the valleys would dry up.
Without Tao, all life would become extinct.
Without Tao, rulers would stumble and fall.

Humility gives us power.
Our leaders should think of themselves as insignificant, powerless,
unworthy of their stature.
Isn't that what humility is all about?

Be strong, but pay no attention to hollow praise.
Don't call attention to yourself.
Don't make a scene.

●

4 0

Tao is always heading back to where it came from.
Tao advances by not pressing forward.

Things exist because they are.
They are because they once were not.

41

When a wise person hears about Tao, he gets right with it.
When an ordinary person hears about Tao,
he tries to get right with it, but eventually gives up.
When a fool hears about Tao, he just laughs and laughs.
If he didn't laugh, it wouldn't be Tao.

Here's what they find so funny:
The path to enlightenment seems covered in shadows.
The way forward feels like taking a step back.
The easiest path seems difficult.
Those with the most virtue seem debased.
Those who are most pure seem to be grubby and soiled.
The deepest thoughts appear shallow.
The greatest strength looks like weakness.
What is most real strikes us as imaginary.
The largest space has no boundaries.
The greatest talent seems to produce nothing.
The greatest voice is unhearable.
The greatest beauty is invisible.

Tao is hidden to us and it has no name.
It is the source and the strength of all things.

●

42

Chapter 42 starts out with some cosmic mumbo-jumbo
about Tao making one,
one making two,
two making three,
and three making everything else.

I don't know what it means. Frankly, I wouldn't worry about it too much.

Let's get to the practical part:
Men hate to be called powerless, insignificant, or unworthy,
but that's how Masters describe themselves.

Because when we lose, we've won.
And when we succeed, we've failed.

Other people will tell you what I'm telling you now:
"Live by the sword, die by the sword."
That's pretty much what Chapter 42 boils down to.
(See Chapter 46 for more details.)

●

43

The softest force in the universe can overcome the hardest of objects.
Something without substance can pass through the space between atoms.

That's how I know about the power of doing nothing.

The silent teachings and the power of doing nothing
can only be understood by a few people.

●

44

What's more important, fame or your well-being?
What's worth more, your money or your life?
What's more dangerous, winning or losing?

If you are too attached to your possessions,
they will bring you misery.
If you hang on to your riches, you will suffer substantial loss.
If you know when you have enough, you will never be disgraced.
If you practice moderation, you can stay out of trouble.

And that's the secret to lasting success.

●

45

The greatest achievements may look like mistakes,
but you will always be able to build upon them.

The fullest reserves may seem empty,
but you will always be able to draw upon them.

The straightest line looks crooked.
The most skilled people come off as clumsy.
The most eloquent people are usually silent.

When it's cold, you can move around to stay warm.
When it's hot, you should keep still and stay cool.
But whatever the weather, if you stay calm,
the world will sort itself out around you.

●

46

"When the world is right with Tao," Lao Tzu said,
"horses haul fertilizer to the fields.
When the world loses touch with Tao, horses are trained for cavalry."

Nothing is more insidious than possession.
Nothing is more dangerous than desire.
Nothing is more disastrous than greed.

If you know when enough is enough, you'll always have enough.

●

47

You don't have to leave your room
to understand what's happening in the world.

You don't have to look out the window to appreciate the beauty of heaven.

The farther you wander, the less you know.

The Masters don't wander around.
They know.
They don't just look.
They understand.
They don't do anything, but the work gets done.

●

4 8

Usually, we try to learn something new every day.

But if we want to get right with Tao,
we have to let go of something every day.

We do less and less, until we end up doing nothing.
And it's when we do nothing that we get the job done.

Let events take their course,
and everything will turn out in your favor.
If you act on your ambitions, they will never pan out.

●

49

The Masters don't make up their minds.
They turn their thoughts to other people.

They are good to good people, and they are good to bad people.
This is real goodness.

They have faith in the faithful, and they have faith in the unfaithful.
This is real faith.

A Master throws himself into the world completely,
forgetting everything he's been told.
People pay attention to him because he lives a life of child-like wonder.

●

5 0

People who look for the secret of long life wind up dead.

Their bodies are the focus of their lives and the source of their death, because they think a healthy body is all there is to life.

Lao Tzu used to say a man who truly understood life
could walk through the jungle without fear
or across a battlefield without armor, totally unarmed.
Wild animals and weapons couldn't kill him.

I know, I know: What's that supposed to mean?
"Well, he couldn't be killed," Lao Tzu said,
"because his body wasn't where he kept his death."

●

5 1

Tao is the source of all living things,
and they are nourished by Tao's power.
They are influenced by the other living things around them,
and they are shaped by their circumstances.

Everything respects Tao and honors its power.
That's just the way it is.

Tao gives life to all things, and its power watches out for them,
cares for them, helps them grow, protects them, and comforts them.

Create something without holding on to it.
Do the work without expecting credit for it.
Lead people without giving them orders.
That's the secret of the power of Tao.

●

5 2

Everything starts with Tao, the mother of all things.
If you know the mother, you know the children.
If you know the children and remember the mother,
you have nothing to fear in your life.

Shut your mouth and keep still, and your life will be full of happiness.
If you talk all the time, always doing something,
your life will be hopeless.

It takes insight to see subtlety.
It takes strength to yield gently to force.
Use that strength to hang on to your insight,
and you will always be at peace.
That's how to get right with Tao.

53

If I had any sense, I'd be trying to get right with Tao,
and the only thing I'd worry about would be messing up.
It's not that hard to get right with Tao,
but people are easily distracted.

"When the king's palace is full of treasure,"
Lao Tzu said, "ordinary people's fields
are smothered with weeds, and the food supplies run out."

Today, you see sharply dressed people
carrying flashy weapons and living the high life.

They own more than they could ever use, let alone need.

They're nothing but gangsters and crooks.
That's not what Tao's about.

54

Tao's power is so deeply entrenched it can never be uprooted.
Tao's power clings so tightly it can never slip away.
It will endure for generations.

If you get in touch with the power of Tao,
it will become real.
If your family gets in touch with the power of Tao,
the power will flourish.

If your community gets in touch with the power of Tao,
the power will grow even stronger.
If your country gets in touch with the power of Tao,
the power will become abundant.

If the world gets in touch with the power of Tao,
the power will be everywhere.

How can I know this?
I just do.

55

A person filled with the power of Tao is like a baby boy:
Bees can't sting him, and wild beasts can't attack him.

A baby has soft bones and weak muscles, but a firm grip.
He hasn't had sex, but he can get an erection.
That's because he's got lots of energy.
He can cry all day and never lose his voice.
That's because he's at one with his world.

If you're at one with the world, you know constancy.
And if you know constancy, you've been enlightened.

It's not healthy to try to prolong your life.
It's unnatural to impose the mind's will upon the body.
People waste time and energy trying to be strong or beautiful,
and their strength and beauty fade.
They've lost touch with Tao, and when you lose touch with Tao,
you might as well be dead.

56

Those who know, don't talk.
Those who talk, don't know.

Shut your mouth.
Be still. Relax.
Let go of your worries.
Stay out of the spotlight.
Be at one with the world and get right with Tao.

If you get right with Tao, you won't be worried
about praise or scorn, about winning or losing,
about honor or disgrace.
That's the way to be.

●

57

You can run a country by sticking to principles,
and you can win a war with strategy and tactics.
But you can gain the entire world by doing nothing at all.

How do I know this? I've seen it happen:
The more restrictions a nation imposes,
the poorer its people become.
When a nation hoards weapons,
troubles arise from within and from without.
When its leaders try to be cunning and clever,
the situation spins further out of control.
When they try to fix things by passing more laws,
they only increase the number of outlaws.

A wise leader says to himself:
"I do nothing, and people transform themselves.
I keep silent, and they do the right thing on their own.
I stay out of the way, and they prosper.
I want for nothing, and they lead simple lives."

●

58

When a nation is ruled with a light touch,
people lead simple lives.
When a government is harsh and demanding,
people will spend their time trying to outsmart it.

Happiness is rooted in misery,
and misery lurks beneath all joy.
Who knows what could happen tomorrow?

Everything is relative;
what's considered proper today may become improper.
Correct appearances may hide dishonesty and sinfulness.

No wonder so many people get confused.

The Masters have sharp minds, not sharp tongues.
They are austere, but never judgmental.
They are straightforward, but not provocative.
They are brilliant, but not flashy.

●

5 9

Leadership is based on moderation.
Practice moderation, and you'll get in touch
with the power of Tao.

If you get right with Tao, nothing is impossible.
If you get right with Tao, there's no limit to what you can do.
If you get right with Tao, you can be a true leader.

Remember this advice if you want to be a leader:
Plant deep roots in firm soil.
Get right with Tao, and you'll always see things clearly.

●

6 0

Being a leader is like cooking a small fish:
Get right with Tao, and it's quick and easy.

When you're in touch with Tao,
you don't need to worry about misfortune.
You can't make it go away, of course,
but you can keep it from harming other people.

Also, as a wise leader, you cause no harm to others,
so people won't have to worry about getting hurt,
and they'll take the opportunity to do the right thing.

●

6 1

Power flows down to every level of existence
like a river to the ocean.

Victory comes from lying perfectly still
and waiting for power to come your way.

If you yield to someone less powerful than yourself,
you will be in a position to influence them.

If you submit to someone more powerful than yourself,
you create an opportunity to get your own way.

So if you want to get ahead, lie low and bide your time.
That way, everybody's happy.

●

6 2

Every living thing gets its strength from Tao.
Good people respect the value of Tao.
The wicked and foolish don't, but Tao provides for them anyway.

Some people gain power and prestige through fancy words,
others through great deeds.
But Tao is available to everyone, not just the powerful.
So don't look down on anybody.

When other people become powerful,
and everybody lines up to kiss their asses,
sit still and stay right with Tao.

Why have the Masters always respected Tao?
Because when you get right with Tao,
you can always find what you need to get by,
and trouble can never find you.

63

Keep still.
Don't work so hard.
Learn to appreciate everyday life.
Pay attention to details.
Start small and work your way up.
When people give you trouble, let it slide.

Break everything down to its essentials.
Get the job done before it becomes a chore.

With the right preparation,
difficult tasks can be completed with ease;
every major project consists of simple steps.

The Masters don't take on more than they can handle,
which is why they can do just about anything.

Don't promise more than you can deliver,
and don't underestimate the task:
You'll only make things harder for yourself.

The Masters are always aware of the difficulties involved,
which is why they never have to deal with them.

● 64

It's easy to maintain balance.
Trouble can be nipped in the bud.
Fragile things break easily, and small things are easy to lose.

Deal with the situation before it becomes a problem.
Keep everything straight so it can't get messed up.

Every tree was once a seed.
Every skyscraper started out with a shovelful of dirt.
And — stop me if you've heard this one before —
a journey of a thousand miles begins with a single step.

When you try too hard, you defeat your own purpose.
Cling to stuff, and you will suffer loss.
The Masters make no effort, so they never fail.
They aren't attached to things, so they never feel loss.

People often screw up when the job's nearly done.
Pay as much attention to the finishing touches
as you do to the initial steps, and you won't screw up like that.

The Masters try to be free from desire.
They don't collect precious things.
They don't cling to any beliefs.
They pay attention to what everybody else ignores.
They help the world get right with Tao,
but don't try to change a thing.

●

6 5

In ancient times, leaders who were right with Tao
didn't teach everybody how to become enlightened.
They kept people's lives simple.

People who know too much can't be taught anything.
Leaders who try to be clever always screw things up.
Leaders who keep things simple always make things right.

If you get that, you'll understand the mysterious power of Tao.

That kind of power is so deep, so extensive,
it penetrates into every level of existence.

●

6 6

An ocean is greater than the hundred rivers that flow into it,
and all it does is wait to receive what they bring.

If you want to teach people, don't talk down to them.
If you want to lead them, find out where they want to go.

People love leaders who make them feel safe
without smothering them.
They'll always support a leader like that,
and because he doesn't try to compete with anybody,
nobody is able to compete with him.

●

67

Everywhere I go, people tell me,
"Tao is so powerful, so immense, it's inconceivable!"

But it's only powerful because it's inconceivable.
If we could wrap our minds around it,
Tao would be just another thing.

The three most important qualities in life
are compassion (showing kindness and mercy to others),
moderation (knowing what a thing is worth),
and modesty (knowing your place in the world).

Courage stems from showing kindness and mercy to others.
Generosity starts with knowing what a thing is worth.
True leadership begins with knowing your place in the world.

These days, though, I see everyone trying to act courageous
without any trace of compassion.
They try to be generous
but they don't practice moderation in their own lives.
They act like leaders, but they have no sense of modesty.
No good can come of this.

If you want to get ahead, show people compassion.
When other people attack you, defend yourself with compassion.
It's the most powerful force in the universe.

●

6 8

A true warrior never uses force with an attitude of pride or anger.
A true victor does not pursue vengeance.
A true leader shows humility.

This is the power of modesty.
It's the best way to deal with people.
It's always been an excellent way to get right with Tao.

●

69

There's an old military saying:
"I'd rather face an attack than have to make one.
I'd rather retreat a foot than try to advance an inch."

That's the secret to moving forward while staying put,
preparing for battle without revealing your strength.

When you defend yourself without any show of force,
you give your opponent nothing to fight.

Attacking an enemy you've underestimated is a costly mistake.
When two forces oppose each other,
the winner is the one most reluctant to fight.

●

7 0

Lao Tzu's advice was easy to understand and easy to follow.
But nobody understood him or did what he suggested.

His words stemmed from ancient wisdom,
and his actions were highly disciplined.
People didn't get that, which is why they didn't understand him.
And the less they understood him,
the more meaningful his advice became.

That's why the Masters live simply,
hiding their wisdom deep within themselves.

●

7 1

If you know what you don't know, you're doing great.
If you don't know what you don't know, you're sick.

The only way to get rid of that sickness is to be sick of it.

The Masters aren't sick, because they got sick of being sick.

●

7 2

When you show no fear at all,
the universe will give you something to really be afraid of.

Don't try to fence people in or grind them down.
Just let them be, and they'll always be on your side.

The Masters know themselves, but they don't reveal themselves.
They love themselves, but they know what their lives are worth.
They let go of all that to concentrate on this.

●

73

Those who dare to be bold die.
Those who dare to be careful survive.
So — what do you want to do?

Why is life like that, you ask?
I don't know.

This is how Tao works:
It doesn't push itself, and it always succeeds.
It acts silently, and it always reacts.
It can't be summoned; it comes whenever it's ready.
It can't be rushed; it's always on time.

"Heaven casts a wide net, with big holes,"
Lao Tzu used to say, "but nothing ever gets by it."

●

74

If people's lives suck, and they look forward to death,
what good does it do to threaten to kill them?

If people are afraid to die, and the wicked are condemned to death,
then who would dare to commit evil?

That doesn't mean you or I
can just take life and death into our own hands.
That'd be like walking up to a buzz saw
and trying to use it without any training.
We'd only end up hurting ourselves.

●

7 5

People starve because the government taxes them to death.
People rebel because the government tries to run their lives.
People act like life is meaningless
because the government takes everything they have.

People who know how to enjoy life
are wiser than people who value their lives.

●

76

A baby's body is soft and gentle.
A corpse is hard and stiff.
Plants and trees are tender and full of sap.
Dead leaves are brittle and dry.

If you are rigid and unyielding, you might as well be dead.
If you are soft and flexible, you are truly alive.

Soldiers trained to fight to the death will die.
A tree that cannot bend with the wind will snap.

Here's a useful saying:
The harder they come, the harder they fall.

Here's another:
The meek shall inherit the earth.

●

77

Lao Tzu said using Tao was like pulling on a bowstring:
The top bends down, the bottom bends up,
and all the energy is focused in the middle.

Tao takes energy from where it is,
and sends it where it needs to be.
But most people take from those who don't have enough,
so those who have too much already can have more.

So who in this world is truly generous to others?
People who are in touch with Tao.
They do their work without taking credit.
They get the job done and move on.
They aren't interested in showing off.

●

7 8

Nothing is softer or more yielding than water.
Yet, given time, it can erode even the hardest stone.
That's how the weak can defeat the strong,
and the supple can win out over the stiff.

Everybody knows it.
So why don't we apply it to our own lives?

Lao Tzu used to say:
"Take on people's problems, and you can be their leader.
Deal with the world's problems, and you'll be a Master."

Sometimes the truth makes no sense.

79

Sometimes, when an argument is settled,
feelings of resentment still remain on either side.
But what's the point of carrying a grudge?

The Masters care about what they owe other people,
not what other people owe them.

People who are in touch with Tao do their duty.
People who aren't try to force others into submission.

Tao doesn't play favorites.
But if you do right by Tao, Tao will do right by you.

●

8 0

Lao Tzu had a dream about a small country with very few people.

They didn't need machines to get their work done faster.
They took their lives seriously, and stayed close to home.

They may have owned boats and carriages,
but they never went anywhere.
They may have owned weapons,
but they kept those weapons locked up, securely hidden.
They had so few responsibilities,
they never had to make a To-Do list to remember what had to be done.

They enjoyed simple foods,
dressed plainly, lived comfortably,
and kept their traditions alive.

And even though their neighbors were so close
they could hear the dogs barking at night,
they had no interest in leaving their homes,
where they grew old peacefully and died.

●

8 1

The truth isn't flashy.
Flashy words aren't true.

Educated people aren't always smart.
Smart people don't always have an education.

Good people don't argue.
People who argue aren't good.

The Masters don't hang on to things.
They're always doing something for other people,
so they always have more to give.
They give away whatever they have,
so what they have is worth more.

Want to get right with Tao? Help other people, don't hurt them.
The Masters always work with people, never against them.

●

A F T E R W O R D

IN THE YEARS since I first discovered the pragmatic wisdom of the Tao Te Ching, my interest in the practical side of personal development (or self-help, or whatever else you'd like to call it) has deepened. I was very fortunate, during my time writing about the publishing industry, to have an opportunity to interview people like organization expert Peter Walsh or entrepreneurial advisor Michael Port, all of whom helped to expand my understanding of personal growth.

At the same time, one of the most frequent questions I got from people who downloaded the previous version of the book you've just read was whether I was ever going to write a "follow-up," and if so where was it going to come from. Some people had specific suggestions, but I never felt that I had anything to add that could improve upon, for example, Marcus Aurelius's *Meditations* with the same modernization tactics I used here.

Eventually, though, I started reading another important text in ancient Chinese philosophy, the I Ching, and though most takes on that book emphasize its role as an oracular tool, where readers can use various randomizing techniques to hit upon one of the 64 trigrams, I was struck by the *sequence* — and it occurred to me the "Book of Changes" (as one of the most apt translations has it) might be an effective handbook for personal transformation if you worked through its chapters in order. (I know: As insights go, this isn't exactly spectacular, but it was news to me at the time, anyway.)

So I started playing with the first few chapters, and I quickly realized that it wasn't going to be as simple as putting a contemporary spin on the fragmentary imagery and commentary on the trigrams and their individual lines. If I wanted to create a practical, straightforward "book of changes," I would have to work my way back to the basic infrastructure and then build something new on top of it.

(Yes, I suppose that *does* sound rather arrogant in retrospect, but I prefer to think of it as ambitious.)

I toyed with the idea of a "64-step program" for a while, but that format never really felt right. Then it occurred to me: If you were trying to make a major change in your life, what would help you make that change? A solid appraisal of your present situation and your capacity for change. And how do you get that appraisal? *Questions.* Starting with one of the biggest: "What do you want from life?"

I started thinking about those 64 questions, but while I was able to figure out what the first 16 or so would be, this was an easy project to set aside as more pressing deadlines came up — especially when it came to thinking about what I would have to *say* about those questions. So I've tinkered with this concept off and on for a while, but it's nowhere near being finished, and I'm not… unless I push myself.

When I started talking with the folks at Channel V Books about publishing *Getting Right with Tao*, they wanted to know what I could offer readers that would make them want to pay for a document that had already been available for free online for more than half a decade. I couldn't think of anything that I could add to this book, anything that was finished, but then I thought: What if I invited the people who bought *Getting Right with Tao* to get a first look at the sequel?

Here's the deal: As this book goes to press, I'm creating a free email newsletter called "I Ching Questions," and I'll use it to write about my conversations with a number of experts on personal and professional development about how we can go about answering the 64 questions I'll be formulating around the chapters of the I Ching, along with my own reflections on those questions. (You'll be able to share your own thoughts and feedback as well.) To subscribe, visit this web page:

http://www.beatrice.com/i-ching-questions.

I won't be promoting this newsletter in any other venues, online or offline; although I can't guarantee that people who haven't bought *Getting Right with Tao* won't discover it eventually, this newsletter is intended just for you, as a way of saying thank you and an invitation to join me in the early stages of an exciting new project.

ACKNOWLEDGMENTS

THE ORIGINAL INSPIRATION for *Getting Right with Tao* came from hanging out on the Internet in the mid-1990s. There are way too many people from that period for me to thank all of them individually, but the relevant members of alt.society.generation-x and alt.religion.kibology know who they are. (But I should take a moment to mention Peter Dubuque, who always made me laugh and who is dearly missed.)

I'd often thought about creating a print edition of this book one day, and Gretel Going and Erin Ferretti Slattery at Channel V Books have done a fantastic job of making that possible. My literary agent, Leslie Daniels, played another essential role in seeing this project through to a successful conclusion.

From the moment in 2001 when I decided to finish writing this book up to the present day, the support of Laura Hogan has been indispensable.

APPENDIX:
The Real Tao Te Ching

AS PROMISED, here are some other English-language versions of Tao Te Ching that are closer to an "authentic" version than what you've just read, if you're interested in learning more about the source material. Of the many editions that I considered as I was working my way through Lao Tzu's 81 chapters, these are among my favorites.

- Stephen Mitchell, first published in 1988. I'm not always 100% sold on Mitchell's tone, and even he admits that it's not an exact translation, but this is probably the best-known version of Lao Tzu in English today, and it is well respected for its straightforwardness and accessibility.

- Brian Browne Walker, first published in 1995. There's a modern oral quality to this version that was a huge inspiration to me, although I've jacked up the contemporary language even further than Walker did.

- Ursula K. Le Guin, first published in 1997. The acclaimed science fiction and fantasy writer hits a sweet spot between classical and modern language, and she also provides illuminating commentary to several chapters.

- David Hinton, first published in 2000. Hinton's poetic language feels (at least to me) very close to what Lao Tzu's advice might have sounded like to his original audience.

- Red Pine, first published in 2001. Pine doesn't just bring his own perspective, which includes several years of living in a Zen monastery, to the text—he also draws upon multiple commentators to put Lao Tzu's words into a broader context.

ABOUT THE AUTHOR

RON HOGAN helped create the literary Internet by launching Beatrice. com in 1995. After several years of writing about the book industry, he recently became the director of e-marketing strategy for a major publisher. He is also the author of *The Stewardess Is Flying the Plane!: American Films of the 1970s.* He lives in New York.